MW01716458

When Mommy and Daddy Divorce

BY
Mary Burchett

Illustrations by Ron Williams

Published in the United States of America
By TATE PUBLISHING,LLC

Book Design by TATE PUBLISHING, LLC.

Printed in the United States of America by
TATE PUBLISHING, LLC
1716 West State Highway 152
Mustang, OK 73064
(888) 361-9473

Publisher's Cataloging in Publication

Burchett, Mary

When Mommy and Daddy Divorce/Mary Burchett

Originally published in Mustang,OK:TATE PUBLISHING:2004

1. Spiritual 2. Children 3. Divorce

ISBN 0-9740939-5-5 $12.95

First Printing: April 2004

Dear Mommy and Daddy,

It was out of my own experience with a grandchild who was hurt through divorce that I decided to write this book. I realize that the child is not the only one hurt in divorce, however, this book was written with your child in mind.

It is my desire to assist you in healing the hurt of your child, who, of course is the innocent victim. It is their world that falls apart without them asking for it.

Child psychologists say that 80% of the children of divorced families have some type of emotional trauma. When divorce occurs, the bond of a family is broken and suddenly the child loses that security that they have had since birth. Many of the children even feel that they are to blame.

Parents need to realize the affect that divorce has on children in order to help their child to adapt. From this understanding will grow a newfound, deep, lasting love that is the foundation of a solid relationship.

It is my hope that as you read this book together, with your child, that healing will come. Just remember that it may take weeks, months, or maybe even years of reassurance for the child to fill the void that has entered his or her life.

May your efforts be rewarded. Wishing you the very best.

Mary Burchett
Author

This book is dedicated to
Jacqui, Mary Rose,
all my grandchildren and
to all the "GRAND" children in the world
who have had to deal with divorce.

Remember—God loves you.

God is everywhere.

God knows everything.

God sees everything.

God loves you.

In the Bible, God says, "I love you with a never ending love."
(Jeremiah 31:3)

Here are two houses.

Mommy lived in one house and Daddy lived in the other.

One day they met,

fell in love

and got married.

They lived in one house and were very happy.

Don't forget-

God is everywhere.

God sees everything.

And God will always love you, no matter what.

Then you were born.

You were made and formed by God.

That means you are very, very special.

Draw a picture about when you were a baby.

After a few years Mommy and Daddy
discovered that their hearts were sore.

Mommy and Daddy started having
disagreements and differences.

Did you feel sad when your parents argued?
Draw a picture of how you felt.

Sometimes when your heart hurts, it causes you to hurt others because you are hurting.

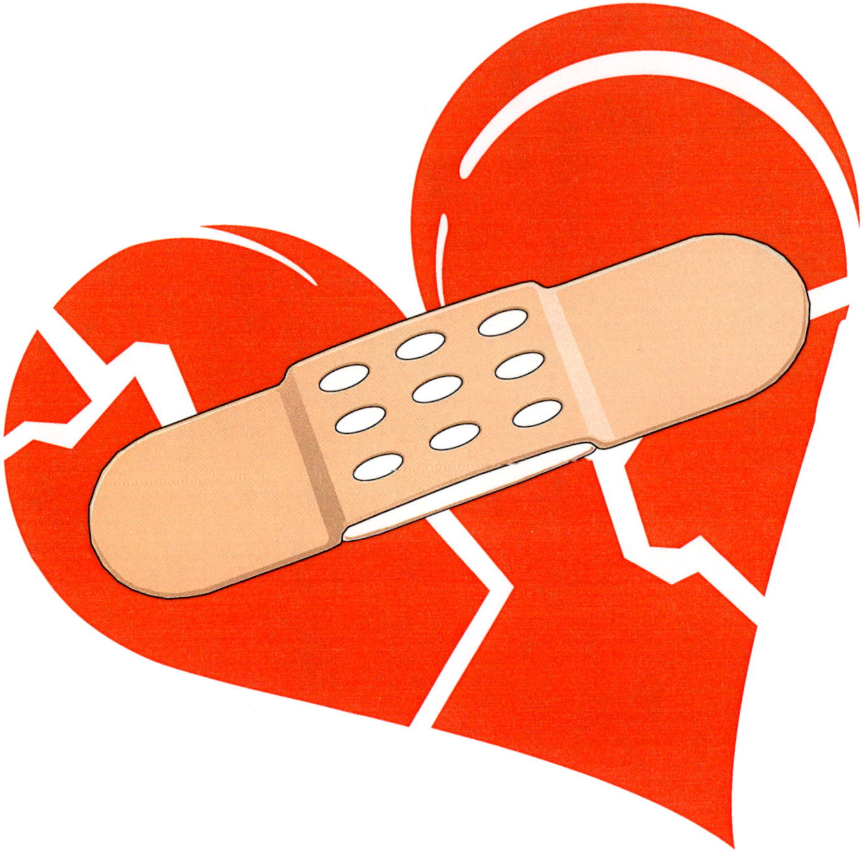

The Bible says in Psalm 147:3, "God heals the broken hearted and bandages their wounds."

Remember-

God is everywhere.
God knows everything.
God sees everything.
God loves you and always will.

Here is a picture drawn by Aren, age 10. She reads her Bible and prays every day for her mommy and daddy.

Draw a picture of you reading your Bible.

Everyone has a heart.

Sometimes your heart gets hurt and is sore like a bruise.
It may not hurt all the time—just when you touch it.

And sometimes it causes a sore,
and the sore leaves a scar.

God knows when you are hurting.

The Bible says, "God looks on the heart."
(I Samuel 16:7)

Here is a picture drawn by Tayler, age 8, and Clytee, age 7. Their friends were sad when their parents got a divorce.

Here is a picture by Michael, 10 years old. He feels very happy, because his friend's parents did not get a divorce.

Do you have a friend whose parents are getting a divorce? Draw a picture of your friend.

Your parents could not agree on the same thing.
Everyone is sad and hurt.

You are caught in the middle.

Mommy

and

Daddy

separate.

They decide to get a divorce.

A divorce means you are no longer married.

Here is a picture drawn by Brooklyn Danielle, age 12.

Draw a picture about how you felt when your world fell apart.

Here is a picture drawn by Jared, age 4.
He thinks a divorce looks like a tornado.

Draw a picture of what divorce looks like to you.

Sometimes when you are little, your heart gets hurt.

Sometimes it hurts when bad things happen to you.

It may hurt for a long time.

Here is a picture by Rachel, age 10.

Everyone is hurt. But you know what?

God can heal the hurt.

He never runs out of love or healing.

He is always with you.

God says in the Bible, "I will never leave you or abandon you."

(Hebrews 13:5)

Draw a picture about how you feel when
you know God's love. He loves you very, very much.

Here is a picture drawn by Taylor M, age 9. He knows God can make you happy again.

Did you know that God has a special angel just for you?

The angel watches over you everywhere you go—
even while you are playing and
even at night while you are asleep.

It doesn't matter where you are,
your angel is watching over you.

Mommy and Daddy both
love you very much.

But now there are two houses again.
Mommy lives in one house
and Daddy lives in the other.

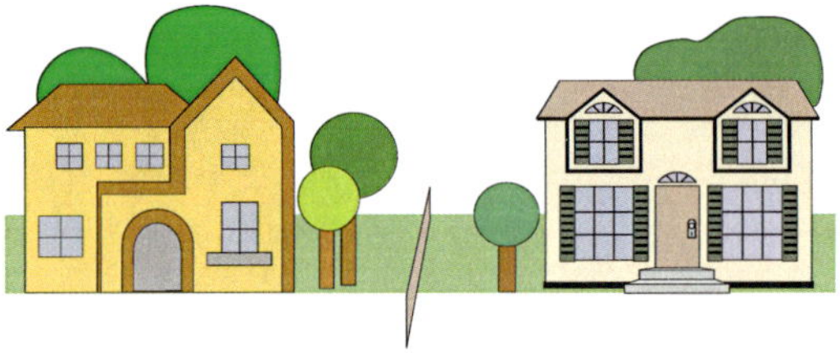

Remember-

God is everywhere. God knows everything.
God sees everything, and God loves everyone.

And remember this-

IT IS NOT YOUR FAULT.

You did nothing wrong.

God and His angels never go to sleep.
They never get tired.
They are always with you day and night.

God will always love you more than anyone in the whole world. God says in Matthew 28:20, "I am with you always, even to the end of the world.

ALWAYS REMEMBER—

God made you special.

You are very important to God.

God is everywhere.

God knows everything.

God sees everything—

AND GOD LOVES YOU!

ACKNOWLEDGEMENTS

Thanks to my wonderful husband, Dwight, and the rest of my family for encouraging me to not give up on this book.

Thanks to Tate Publishing who fell in love with my book and gave me guidance, suggestions and wonderful ideas to help me get this book published.

Thanks to Ron Williams, a top artist who did a superb job on the artwork.

Thanks to all my little artists who also did a fantastic job—Brooklyn Danielle, Tayler, Clytee, Taylor, Rachel, Michael, Jared and Aren.

Thanks to all the wonderful people who have endorsed my book.

And last, but not least, thank you for purchasing this book. May it bring healing to your family.

To order more copies of *When Mommy and Daddy Divorce*
contact author at:

Mary Burchett
6801 S. Anderson Rd.
Oklahoma City, OK 73150

or

TATE PUBLISHING, LLC

1716 West State Highway 152
Mustang, Oklahoma 73064

(888) 361 - 9473

TATE PUBLISHING, LLC

www.tatepublishing.com